ON THE DOORSTEP
OF THE CASTLE

Also by Elizabeth Clark-Stern

Out of the Shadows
A Story of Toni Wolff and Emma Jung
ISBN 978-0981393940

Soul Stories
Safari to Mara and Aria of the Horned Toad
ISBN 978-1926975009

ON THE DOORSTEP
OF THE CASTLE

A play of Teresa of Avila
and Alma de Leon

Elizabeth Clark-Stern

il piccolo editions
by
fisher king press

Published by
il piccolo editions an imprint of Fisher King Press
www.fisherkingpress.com
info@fisherkingpress.com
1-800-228-9316 Toll free Canada & the US
+1-831-238-7799 International

On the Doorstep of the Castle
Copyright © 2013 Elizabeth Clark-Stern
ISBN 978-1-77169-002-7
First Edition

Published simultaneously in Canada, the United Kingdom, and the United States of America. For information on obtaining permission for use of material from this work, please submit a written request to: permissions@fisherkingpress.com

Cover image "All Good Things Come to Us Through Her" is an art work used with permission by Patrice M. Donohue of Seattle, Washington.

Cover design by Sean Juen
www.iwigwam.com

ACKNOWLEDGMENTS

Many people gave their talent, love and support to make this book possible.

To the C.G.Jung Society Seattle, the Jungian Psychotherapist Association, and the Northwest Alliance for Psychoanalytic Study, for their support of the arts, and my work

to Lee Roloff and Susan Scott, for artistic and soul-nourishing support

to Lindsey Rosen, who first played Alma in my mind and provided the image of a powerful, soulful, artist woman who became the character

to Patrice Donahue for her support, hard work, and the beautiful art work photographed for our cover

to Ken Kimmel, Barb Morgan, Bunny Brown and Diane Bogue for their support

to Constance Romero, Jungian analyst and director of the New Orleans Archetypal Theater Company, and to Susan Welch, pianist and director of the New Orleans Jung Society, for bringing us to New Orleans. Your loving attention and professional support for *Out of the Shadows* inspired the writing of this play

a mighty debt of gratitude to Brent Robinett for sound recording

much love and gratitude to the multi-gifted Laura Shea for design and execution of the costumes to Donna Lee, with love, for her friendship and dedication through all the years

to Aylee Welch, and Beverly Olevin for script feedback and support

a world of love and gratitude to Patty Cabanas and Mel Mathews, my editor and publisher, for their support, ideas, and love

and, most importantly, great love and gratitude to my husband, John, for everything.

Dedicated to Lindsey Rosen's daughter, Laila Rosen, and to my grand-daughter, Dylan Hansen, young dancers whose joy and uniqueness will help make the Twenty-first century the Century of Women.

CHARACTERS

Alma de Leon, age 20-40
Teresa of Avila, age 42-62

TIME

1559-1579

SETTINGS

A street in Avila, Spain

The Convent of the Incarnation, Avila

Small room in the secret house in San Roche, a district outside
Avila

The Discalced convent of Saint Joseph, San Roche

On the road across the plains of La Mancha

A town square

A room in the town's newly-founded Discalced convent

Convent of the Incarnation, Avila

Convent of Saint Joseph, San Roche

On the balcony, Convent of the Incarnation

PRODUCTION NOTE: While the original production fea-
tured dance as a central element, and a full production is op-
timal, the play can be performed as a reading. In such cases
it can be read on book, either staged or on podiums, the text
providing its own "dance" of symbol, theme, and characteriza-
tion.

ORIGINAL CAST

Alma de Leon: Lindsey Rosen

Teresa of Avila: Elizabeth Clark-Stern

DESIGN AND TECHNICAL SUPPORT

Stage Manager and Sound Operation:
Donna Lee

Sound Recording:
Brent Robinett

Costume research, design, and construction:
Laura Shea

Choreography, stage movement, and direction:
Anna Mansbridge

Lighting Design and Operation:
John Stern

Script Consultation:
John Stern, Susan Scott, Aylee Welch

ACT ONE

In the darkness, a classical Spanish guitar: energy, pathos, inquiry.

Lights fade up on a bare stag with two chairs, and a rope spread across the back wall. The rope is adorned with single sheets of parchment, like flags on a clothesline.

Alma enters, dancing an expression of longing, loss, and hope.

As the dance concludes, she unclips a sheet of parchment from the hanging rope, and moves downstage, reading her letter to herself.

ALMA:

> The year of our Lord 1559. Saludo, Teresa Sanchez. They say you are the most awake woman in Spain. I must be completely truthful with you. If I am to be admitted to the Order of the Incarnation, there must be no secrets between us.
>
> *Aside.*
>
> Do I dare write what my father whispered to me, of Teresa's own blood? . . . No.
>
> *Back to the letter.*
>
> I find myself entering my twentieth year with great hunger for something I can believe in whole-heartedly. I am awed by the new revelations of Copernicus. The earth beneath our feet *moves*, ever turning toward the sun. It may be that soon, mankind can use our own minds to explain the vast reaches of the "out there" . . . But what of the "in here?" I am plagued by an aridity of soul, I attempt to pray. I think, "What for? Who is listening?"
>
> *Aside.*

She will toss my letter out the window, crying, "Who is this godless child?"

Returning to the letter.

I am called Alma de Leon, my family descended from Moses de Leon, author of *The Zohar*, the sacred, forbidden book of the Kabbalah. I am proud of my Jewish blood, although, at the insistence of the Inquisition, our family was baptized in the service of our Lord Jesus Christ. We bore the shame, and the poverty of the *conversos*. In my family, we ate pork, so great was our fear we would be boiled in oil, for abstaining.

A breath, dispelling memory. Back to the letter.

So why do I petition to be a novice in your care? It was the *stories*, whispered across the arid plains, "There is a woman who receives raptures directly from God." I did not believe this. I had to see for myself. When I arrived in Avila, a crowd had gathered in the square, the scorching wind blowing dust into our eyes. "What are you waiting for?" I asked. "You will see," said an old woman next to me. I scoffed, "Does this nun see God every day at high noon?" She shrugged. "Sometimes. You never know." I followed her gaze into the dust. There I saw you, walking matter-of-factly with your sisters, your fine robes whipping behind you like a sail on a mighty ship . . . Then, I saw your gait slow down, your arms grow limp, your face distort in pain, yet, through your eyes, a seeing far beyond. You giggled, whispered, sighed, your feet moving upward, as if climbing an unseen staircase. Up, up, you stepped, your feet floating off the ground. The sisters pulled you down, lest you float away. I knelt in the streaming

4

dust. You passed, muttering, "We are not angels, we have bodies." That dear, ordinary voice struck me to the core. Lifting off the earth is so common to you, as I would stub a toe . . . I want to see what you see, know what you know.

Lights fade. Alma places the letter on the seat of a chair and exits.

Music. Classical Spanish guitar: reaching for comfort while churning within.

Lights find Teresa, in a state of worry. She places the chairs facing one another, but askew.

> *She takes Alma's letter from the chair, reading it with anxiety, pacing the floor.*
>
> *KNOCK off stage.*
>
> *Teresa is startled, holds the letter to her breast, summoning courage.*
>
> *KNOCK again.*

TERESA:
Entrada!

Alma enters, beholds Teresa.

There is a moment of silence, apprehension.

Alma falls to her knees before Teresa.

ALMA:
Mother—

TERESA:

> Stand tall, girl. Our Lord deserves such prostrations, not I. And, I am no Mother Superior. Some would say I am too insane, too swept away by raptures, for such an office. Sit.

> *Alma sits in a chair opposite Teresa.*

> *Teresa studies the letter.*

> You make a passionate appeal, yet I doubt you have any idea what strict requirements we have here. Mortification, thrice weekly—

ALMA:

> I doubt you comprehend how harshly the world has dealt with me and my family. What is the blood of the lash, compared with exile, execution.

> *Teresa falls into silence.*

> *Alma's eyes anxiously scan the room.*

> You have so many beautiful things. That landscape.

TERESA:

> The plains of La Mancha.

ALMA:

> It captures the fragile essence of our wild, arid, country. The red blooms of the limberbush, reaching to the sky. I did not expect such luxury. As I walked through your halls, I passed nuns in fine jewels.

TERESA:

> Many of the sisters here, like myself, defied their families to enter the Order. I slipped away in the middle of the night, arriving here with nothing. My father could not countenance his beloved Teresita

living in austerity. He insisted I have private quarters, my own kitchen, fine paintings. My mother died when I was quite young. How could I refuse him?

ALMA:

I am most interested in the history of your family.

TERESA:

This interview is not about me. I am curious why a *converso* desires to become a Carmelite nun.

ALMA:

"Carmelite." Such a lovely name. From the hermits of Mount Carmel, in the holy land. It is said they drank water from the fountain of Elijah, lived on berries, their only concern, love. I have a cousin called Elijah. He fled in exile to Jerusalem when we were but thirteen. His family refused to submit to conversion.

TERESA:

I am sorry for them. I have worked very hard to educate our Jews on the sacred teachings of our Lord, Jesus the Christ.

ALMA:

I deeply envy the integrity, the courage of my Eli. I have neither. I buried my mother this year, my father the year before. Our small house, our pigs, our chickens were taken from me to pay the *converso* death tax. I have no dowry, only my strong woman's body. I do not think you want my arid soul, but it is here as well, hungry for my own rapture, even as another voice within me scoffs at such a notion.

TERESA:

You would have to sleep in the dorm with the other poor nuns, clear tables—

ALMA:
(*desperately*)

> I will scrub the floors every day. Do you not understand? I have no *home*.

> You will fight for me, with the Mother Superior?

TERESA:
(*moving away, distracted*)

> The almond blossom is in bloom. I cannot run through orchards, showered in white petals. You can, this day.

> *Alma waits, hoping for a better answer.*

> *Teresa responds with aversion.*

> Go! Go!

> *Alma hurries from the room.*

> *Teresa shivers, her breath quickening.*

> *She touches her breast, addressing an inner Presence.*

> My dearest Lord, you are here . . . How strong and healthy you are, your face burned by the sun . . . You have been building a house? . . . A house for a Jewish family . . . How can I fight for this girl? She knows who I am! . . . What if she tells the world? The Inquisition, the Pope will dance at my demise. I can feel the boiling oil on my skin . . . Yes, I leap to the tragic. It is one of my greatest faults . . . You want me to fight for her . . . I owe it to her . . . Yes, my Lord, You know what it is, to be an outcast Jew . . . Oh, my dearest, how am I to atone for my sin? . . . Take off my shoes?

She looks at her feet, puzzled.

Lights fade.

Music; a guitar of longing.

Lights fade up. Alma enters, wearing the veil of a novice. She carries a book beneath her arm. She places it aside and she scrubs the floor with a worn cloth.

Music fades into silence.

    Alma sits on her heels, wiping her brow, adjusting the veil.

ALMA:
(addressing the heavens)

> Mama and Papa, yes, it is me. From *converso* to Carmelite. I scarcely recognize myself when I chance to look in a glass, and yet, on the rare occasions when I walk the streets of Avila with the other sisters, people smile at me, look into my eyes with respect, even joy, gratitude. Some bow as I walk forth to haul water from the well. Old gentlemen take my bucket and talk to me, as if I am wise, simply because I wear this itchy veil. It fits me ill. I use the slightest excuse to take it off. My soul, my body, revel in the fortress of esteem within these wall, but the hairs on my head? They cry, "Who are you, Alma de Leon? What have you done?"

TERESA:
(Off Stage, ringing a prayer bell)

> Alma de Leon, we await your presence at morning prayer.

Alma sets aside her scrubbing rag, and fetches her book. She kneels, facing the audience, as if looking out a window. She opens to a page, and bows her head.

Teresa enters, exasperated. She is quite surprised to find Alma in private prayer.

Teresa peeks at the book, gasps, reaches for it.

ALMA:

(seizing the book)

> No—

TERESA:

> You *have* it! I am struck blind with envy. My copy of *The Third Spiritual Alphabet* was impounded by the Inquisition, branded heresy for teaching people to pray *in private*. Where did you get it?

ALMA:

> A gift from a homeless man to whom I gave shelter and soup. A Muslim who could not practice his faith, but took comfort in learning to pray by breathing, chanting "aleph, bet, gimmel." I set up an altar in the corner of our chicken coop. I work so hard, breathing, counting, but my mind is like a wild donkey, braying and kicking.

TERESA:

> I used to say I had tiny moths flying about in my mind. Or worse, a madman loose in the house. What instructions do you give your mind, as you pray?

ALMA:

> To see the figure of our Lord Christ.

TERESA:

Only picture him?

ALMA:

What else?

TERESA:

I did this myself, for many years, only praying to a passive mental image. Then, one day, I allowed myself to stop constructing pictures, and simply *know* his reality. I was close beside him, as he knelt in the garden of Gethsemane. I felt what he was feeling. A depth of love and compassion flowed from me. I wanted to soothe his agony, wipe the sweat from his brow. Thereafter, when I prayed, I was with him in this way. It was still twenty years before my first rapture—

ALMA:

So *long?*

TERESA:

Apparently, God wanted me to wait. You must try this, surrendering to the active reality of Christ in your mind.

ALMA:

Is this not all a conjure of the imagination?

TERESA:

Valgame Dios! They are as different as the night the day. When my little mind thinks to fashion a colloquy with God, it is like scratches on parchment, all froth and fantasy. When the rapture captures me, unbidden, the Voice echoes with all the chords of eternity, my mind awake as the sky at dawn.

Noticing Alma's gentle attention.

And, sister, how can you expect transformation kneeling here in the hallway, before a draughty window? Does this impersonate your chicken coop?

ALMA:

I must have light. And, yes, solitude. I cannot pray shut up in a window-less room with all the other sisters, chanting all that Latin! From here I can see the garden and the streets beyond. See children running, red ribbons streaming behind them in the sun. This same sun shines on the streets of the children in Leon, where there is great need. Mama used to say, "Alma, find yourself outside yourself, as the earth encircles the sun."

TERESA:

I envy that your mother lived so long.

ALMA:

She would disagree, so great was her suffering.

TERESA:

(sinking into her own guilt; turning this darkness onto Alma)

It is reported that you consider yourself above weekly mortification.

ALMA:

I thought it would not matter to me, that I could apply the lash with all the others.
Perhaps it feels redundant.

TERESA:

It smacks of pride.

ALMA:

Yes, no doubt. The tiny kernel of it I have left. Do not take it from me.

TERESA:

And if I make an example of you, shame you before God and everyone?

ALMA:

(gravely)

I would not do that, if I were you.

Teresa allows the timber of the threat to penetrate.

TERESA:

Do as you will!

Teresa runs off.

Alma smiles.

Lights fade. Music of torment.

Light finds Teresa, draped across two chairs, alone, in her oratory. She stares off, in a trance.

KNOCK off stage.

Teresa does not respond.

KNOCK repeats. Teresa hears it, but her awareness of the sound is subtle.

ALMA:

(off stage)

Sister Teresa. It is I, Alma de Leon.

Teresa looks up, vaguely.

Are you ill?

No response.

Sister Teresa?

No response.

Alma enters, takes in Teresa's dazed and debilitated state.

What has happened?

Teresa struggles to make eye contact with Alma.

Sister, you frighten us all. No one has seen you for days. Sister Teresa, can you hear me? I come with a motive of my own. I do not know where else to turn.

Alma takes Teresa's hands.

Your hands are cold as the snow on Mount Carmel. Should I fetch a physician?

TERESA:
What ails me cannot be cured by the science of man.

ALMA:
What is your disease?

TERESA:
(moaning, closing her eyes, in pain and ecstasy)
Dear Lord, again?

ALMA:
What do you feel, entering your soul?

14

TERESA:

An angel, in bodily form, not tall, but short and very beautiful, his face so aflame that he appears to be one of the highest types of angels . . . In his hands a long golden spear, at the end of the iron tip, a point of fire.

She cries out.

With this spear he pierces my heart so that it penetrates to my entrails. When he draws it out, I think he is drawing them out with it . . . He leaves me completely afire with a great love for God.[1]

Teresa collapses in an exhaustion of ecstasy and agony.

Teresa notices Alma.

I am so alone in this. My father confessors do not want to hear it. They fear it is the work of the devil, or madness, or they simply do not know what to do with me.

ALMA:

I am so sorry.

TERESA:

"Write it down, Teresa," chime my confessors. Surely they want proof of my heresy, for the Bishops of the Inquisition.

ALMA:

What does your Lord Christ say of this?

TERESA:

He too is unrelenting: "Lift your quill, Teresa. Be my scribe."

ALMA:

Have you attempted it?

TERESA:

I am a woman. To write a book, I should be an educated man.

ALMA:

No man has experienced what you have. Just now, as you spoke, you painted a picture for me. I saw the gleam in the eyes of this short angel as he plunged the spear into your heart.

Alma fetches quill and paper from the rope; gives these to Teresa.

Write it now, just as you described it, word by word.

Teresa sighs, trembles, takes the parchment and a quill, kneels, and places them on the seat of her chair as a makeshift desk.

TERESA:

Thank you.

(studying Alma's face)

I seem to remember, you were distressed when you came in.

ALMA:

It is nothing.

TERESA:

Tell me.

ALMA:

(emotion coming forth)

I have been so terribly lonely, Sister Teresa. If you but knew. I pray and pray and feel nothing. I had to take some action. I thought only to emulate the hermits of Mount Carmel, yet I am chastised.

TERESA:

What is your offense?

ALMA:

I took the remains of our wealthy sisters' sumptuous dinners, to the poor.

Teresa is amazed.

I walked to the district of San Roche, just outside walls of Avila. There the people are in great need: *conversos*, poor Catholics, Muslims in hiding. Oh, sister Teresa, the children had never seen a pomegranate, much less tasted partridge.

Teresa bursts into wild, exuberant laughter.

You find me a figure of sport?

TERESA:

No, no—

(laughing joyously)

God is great! He sends a foxy little angel to puncture me again and again, opening my heart to your good work. What you have done, is worth ten thousand raptures!

Alma is awash with relief.

I am mortified that you are surrounded by peacocks and popinjays. Come, after supper tonight, we will both steal away to San Roche, with all the luxuries of my table, and you will teach me what it is, to love the poor.

Lights fade. Teresa exits.

Music, of discovery, of home.

Light finds Alma, plucking a letter from the rope. She moves downstage, reading it.

ALMA:

The year 1562, Dearest cousin Eli,

Aside.

What if this letter is captured? I would be in great danger. I must find courage, and trust that it will be delivered *converso to converso,* along the secret highway of the Jews—all the way to Jerusalem.

Back to the letter.

Cousin Eli, do you remember me? I saw you last, that terrible day, when we were but thirteen. They dragged you away, with your whole family. I wanted to go with you, into exile. Mama and Papa held me down. Your face still lives in my mind. And what of me? I have become part of a movement for Reform of the Carmelite Order, that has all of Avila in an uproar. Sister Teresa has become impassioned with the dream that we can follow in the way of the great Saint Francis of Assisi. The city fathers—and the church friars, cry "Foul!" Some say we are mad! We are far from insane. We ask not one penny from church or state. We will live on our sewing, wear rough garments and no shoes. Forgive me, Eli, I go on and on about myself! I want you to know that when I pray, of late, I see you, as a man, black of beard and tall of stature, walking through the streets of Jerusalem, the frayed ends of your prayer shawl lifting in the breeze. It was you who told me that the word Kabbalah means "reception"—the Jews lay out a reception for the divine, as for a wedding feast . . .

TERESA:
(off stage, in great distress)

Alma de Leon!

Alma quickly hides the letter.

Alma de Leon!

Teresa enters, trembling with stark terror.

ALMA:

Are you ill?

TERESA:

We must abandon this insanity.

ALMA:

Sit. I will fetch water.

TERESA:
(her eyes wild with a vision)

No! We must go. Now.

ALMA:

The Grand Inquisitor knocks on our door?

TERESA:

No. The devil here on my left side. A great flame pours from his body into mine! His voice snarls in my head, as if in despair[2]—as if his great loneliness could only be assuaged by destroying me . . . We must abandon this accursed Reform. Leave this wretched house before the Pope, the Inquisitors discover what we have done!

ALMA:

You let this Devil turn you away from yourself!

TERESA:

"Let him?" I have no will!

ALMA:

You do. You conjure him in your mind.

TERESA:

It is *you* be-devil me. This secret you hold over me. . . Be Gone! Take your Devil with you!

Alma exits.

Silence.

Teresa continues to cower at the "devil."

ALMA:
(off stage)

Is he gone?

TERESA:

No!

Alma returns.

ALMA:

I see nothing but a woman, afraid. When we open our doors this day, you will be Mother Superior, prioress of the Carmelite Discalced Order of Saint Joseph. I, and all the world, will address you as "Mother."

TERESA:

I am unworthy.

ALMA:

Stop it, Mother Teresa of Jesus. Call forth your mentor, Saint Francis of Assisi.

TERESA:

Ah, perhaps I could . . .

(calling to the Heavens)

Saint Francis, wise one, grace us with your transcendent presence.

Silence.

ALMA:

He does not come. He wants you to stand down this fear, with your own self.

TERESA:
(in agony)

Do you not fear Hell?

ALMA:

I have *been* there. For my people, Hell is right here on this earth. What do you fear, Mother? Your own might? Or do you look upon the bare walls of our austere new home, secretly longing for the luxury you left behind?

Teresa trembles, yet sees the wisdom of it.

She stands tall, addressing the devil on her left side.

TERESA:

El Monstruo, Devil, shame on you, for scaring a poor woman. Today, as the sun rises, we will open the doors of our new home. Saint Joseph's of the Discalced, the barefoot Carmelites.

Silence.

He is gone. He will return.

ALMA:

He does so at his own peril.

TERESA:
(studying Alma's face)

Why is this so important to you, *converso?*

ALMA:

I must still wear a scratchy veil. At least now, I can lose my shoes.

TERESA:

You will not tell me. So. So.

Music. A luminous Spanish guitar.

Teresa and Alma move in a sacred ritual.

Teresa sits, as Alma removes Teresa's shoes.

Alma sits, and Teresa removes Alma's shoes.

Alma helps Teresa remove her golden cape. Both women now wear a rustic brown tunic and black veil. Teresa's face is framed with her white wimple, but it too is modest. Alma wears only the veil of a novice.

They form a procession, one behind the other.

Teresa rings a small hand bell as they walk down stage.

the friars in Toledo are eager to read it. Beyond their eyes, the Inquisition, the Pope.

ALMA:

It is an honest work. People will rejoice that it is possible to have so personal a relationship, with God.

TERESA:

And you?

ALMA:

(taking the book gently from Teresa, opening a page, reading)

I have many favorite passages . . . "The Godhead is like a very clear diamond, much larger than the whole world . . . All we do is seen in this diamond, every facet in the depth of our souls."[3] When I read your pages, I believe that one day, such vision may be possible for me also.

TERESA:

Alma de Leon, I have selected you to carry my manuscript to the fathers in Toledo.

ALMA:

Me?

TERESA:

Of all the sisters at Saint Joseph's, you have the greatest understanding of my work.

Alma is amazed.

And, an added honor: you must stop in Madrid to give my regards to King Philip.

ALMA:

The King? Why would he receive me, a *converso?*

TERESA:

You are my ambassador. He knows me from the esteem of my family, from our work here.

ALMA:

You are too terrified to take the book yourself. "Send the converso, she is expendable!"

TERESA:

Philip is more monk than monarch. He will only look at your feet.

Alma is not convinced.

It is my neck beneath the blade, not yours.

ALMA:

I do not believe that.

TERESA:

Will you do this for me? My motives are not always obvious. They are like the earth, moving, as you often remind me, around the sun. Yet we cannot feel it.

ALMA:

I do feel it sometimes, late at night. The motion, beneath my bare feet. Perhaps it is only a dream.

Bowing, with formality.

I will do this for you.

Teresa is quite pleased; gives her the book.

You are requiring me to trust you. I cannot, but I too have motives buried beneath the earth.

(looking around)

26

I am loathe to leave these walls, even for a temporary sojourn. I have a life here I could never have imagined: praying, dancing, singing.

TERESA:

It will be here, when you come home.

Alma goes.

Teresa feels something swirling within her.

TERESA:

You! Writing Devil!

Swatting her left side.

The wretched book is *gone*. She took it away. You can torment me no more with your prattle.

Teresa turns to her right, in the voice of "the devil."

"A woman, writing of her private discourse with God? They will burn you alive!"

As herself, smacking her left side.

Hah! No more! Out!

She laughs, swatting the devil as the lights fade.

Regal music heralds Alma's entrance to the court.

Lights fade up as Alma enters, clutching Teresa's book as she walks bravely forth, bowing deeply, addressing the audience as "King Philip."

ALMA:

Your majesty . . .

(glancing at her feet, with a smile)

My feet are very well, thank you . . . Yes, our Mother
Teresa of Jesus is very well. She sends her deepest
regards, and thanks your majesty for your support of
our Reform convent, Saint Joseph's. She said "King
Philip would make a very fine monk" . . . ah, you also
aspire to run barefoot?

She laughs, then listens.

Do *I* know about the feminine face of God?

She is amazed.

. . . You call her Sophia?

(whispering)

From the forbidden Gnostic text? . . . You are truly a
remarkable man.

(regarding the book beneath her arm)

Yes, this is Mother Teresa of Jesus' autobiography. I
am to deliver it to the church fathers, in Toledo . . .
Yes, Mother is terrified. She fears they required her
to write it to prove her heresy to the Inquisitors . . .
You also fear the power of the church? Can you not
prevail over the Pope? . . . Yes, I am young in the ways
of the world, but stubborn enough to believe we can
change it . . . You want to read her book . . . Very well,
only for the afternoon . . . You will pray to Sophia, to
send me what I am searching for? How did you know
I was searching? Ah . . . you are searching as well.

Alma goes.

Lights fade.

Music in the darkness: a guitar filled with promise.

Lights find Alma, scrubbing the floor.

> *Teresa plucks a letter from the rope, reads it with animation as she hurries to Alma.*

TERESA:

Alma de Leon, what did you say to the King?

ALMA:
(frightened)

Nothing of consequence.

TERESA:

You transfigured him. How did you do it?

ALMA:

I gave him your book.

TERESA:

Then, we are both culpable!

ALMA:

What will they do to us?

TERESA:
(laughing)

Our great King Philip came down from his throne, assembled a meeting of all the church fathers. He told them the austerity of our Reform embodies the ideal of the Pope himself. A brilliant tactical maneuver! The church fathers were humbled.

(reading from the letter)

They write: "Teresa of Jesus, you are ordered to take to the road. Establish as many Discalced convents as there are hairs on your head!"[4]

ALMA:

Take to the road, in the manner of Saint Francis?

TERESA:

In the manner of *us*! Young women all across Spain will feel the passion of our love for God, for the poor. They will burn their shoes, and run to us!

Teresa seizes Alma's hands.

Lively music accompanies Alma and Teresa, as they do a joyous folk dance.

As the dance ends, lights fade.

ACT TWO

In the darkness, a guitar in a minor key tells the story of hardship, struggle.

CRACK of a whip hitting the hide of a mule.

Lights find Alma and Teresa, perched in a "mule cart" made of two chairs. Teresa faces forward. Alma is behind her, facing upstage.

TERESA:
(addressing the unseen character of the Muleteer in front of her)

Pablo, our weary mules cannot find the road in the dark, however savagely you beat them!

ALMA:

May I come out? I cook like a pie in an oven.

TERESA:

We are an enclosed Order, even on the road. I will not have it appear that the sisters in my convents are my "daughters." That is very effeminate. I want you to be a strong man.[5]

ALMA:

I cannot breathe.

TERESA:

Emerge, if you must. But only I may address the muleteer.

ALMA:
(turning around, placing the chair beside Teresa, sitting to face forward)

A blister of stars, like sunlight through the close threads of my mother's wedding veil.

A gentle despair.

I thought to escape the life of a wandering Jew.

33

To Teresa

Do you not long for the peace of our beloved Saint Joseph's? You were kinder there. I fear the power of your office has made a melon of your head.

TERESA:

A melon? If you accuse me of vanity, I accept the charge. I confess, I thrive on this life! I no longer feel the sting of envy for my brothers, conquistadors in the Americas. I have my own war in every town, the fat friars terrified we will shave tithing from their coffers!

ALMA:

Your enemies call you *andariega:* vagabond. I fear for your safety.

TERESA:

I did not force you to come with me.

ALMA:

I had to.

TERESA:

You did not.

ALMA:

I could not be at Saint Joseph's without you.

TERESA:

The heat has driven you mad.

ALMA:

Yes, surely that is it.

TERESA:

Go back, then.

ALMA:
(*desperately*)

> Are you so blind? I cannot be anywhere in the world without you. I thought to learn from you, not to need you.

Silence.

TERESA:
(*addressing the Muleteer*)

> Pablo, stop. We will sleep this night cloistered beneath the stars.

Teresa gets out of the cart.

Alma does not move.

(*to "Pablo"*)

> Yes, yes, no fires. Bandits might steal our rosaries! Go, tend the mules.

Teresa studies Alma.

> I did not know the magnitude of your feelings.

ALMA:

> I have been cowed by your magnificence, longing for you to give me a mother's love.

Allowing the rage.

> I feel a great torrent rising within me . . . I know who you are, Teresa Sanchez.

> How if I tell the whole world what I know from the lips of my own father? Your grandfather, Juan Sanchez—a Jew, whipped, chased naked in the streets of Toledo. He ran from his shame, to Avila; made his

fortune, and bought himself a certificate testifying to his pure Spanish blood. You grew up in wealth, a Spanish aristocrat hiding your true self, while I suffered the shame of my identity.

TERESA:

The devil speaks in you.

ALMA:

No, it is me, myself. This night, I hate you. I could take your very life, and be glad of it!

Alma weeps.

TERESA:
(sitting beside Alma in the cart, softly)

What manner of woman was she, your mother?

ALMA:

. . . Worn. Her face etched with worry. Her eyes flittered about, ever terrified of what lurked in the next moment. The crackle of an ember in the fireplace, a random breaking of a glass, her body jerked. I looked for myself in her eyes. She was elsewhere.

TERESA:

I grieve for you, for her. I have wondered if my mother did not suffer similar agonies, but all I saw was her beautiful, smiling face.

ALMA:

To please can be its own disease.

TERESA:

I know that poison well.

ALMA:

(taking out a shawl)

> The *tallis*, prayer shawl of my grandfather, Abraham de Leon. My mother had only just washed it the morning they came and took him away. She wore it beneath her clothes, as we stood, watching them tie him to the stake, and light the fire.

TERESA:

> You saw it?

ALMA:

> My eyes were shielded by my mother's arms. I could smell it. I can still smell it.

TERESA:

> What was his "crime?"

ALMA:

> Teaching Kabbalah to *conversos*.

TERESA:

(addressing the shawl reverently)

> I mourn for your grandfather, Abraham de Leon.
>
> How can such things happen in this world?

ALMA:

> Ask your Lord.

TERESA:

> It is not my place.

ALMA:

> You ask him everything else.

TERESA:

> He is not at my beck and call.

ALMA:

You are afraid even He does not know the answer.

Teresa kneels, closes her eyes.

TERESA:

Dearest Lord, what is the meaning of the suffering of sister Alma de Leon?

Silence.

Teresa opens her eyes, in awe.

ALMA:

What is it?

TERESA:

He wants to hear from *you.*

ALMA:

I have no gift for rapture.

TERESA:

Apparently our Lord thinks otherwise.

Alma wraps the prayer shawl around her shoulders.

ALMA:

Oh, Lord, if you can manage it, show me *why.*

Alma breathes slowly, clutching the tallis to her breast.

Silence.

At last, Alma opens her eyes, startled. She cries out, seeing an inner vision that is at once terrifying and so compelling no amount of fear can make her turn away from it. She follows the inner vision until her quick breathing slows down.

"Mend, and fight . . . ?"

TERESA:

His words?

ALMA:

Not a "Him." I felt the presence of Her, just now, within me, the body of a beautiful woman with long dark hair, impaled upon a tree, its trunk split in two— Her body ripped asunder . . . She reached for the disparate branches, to pull them back together.

TERESA:

"Mend, and fight?"

ALMA:

There were other words, carved on the severed branches, as from an ancient hand. "Power" on the left branch; "Love" on the right one . . . (*in torment*) Is this not the evil in my own self? Just now, I had no power to inspire your love, so was ready destroy you, to cry to the world, "Teresa of Jesus is a Jew!"

TERESA:

You are ever my teacher. I too have torn asunder Power and Love: Mother Superior of the melon-head. I have pushed you out of my heart, the *Jew*, as I have pushed away the Jew in my own self. I believe this vision is our Shekhinah, the feminine face of our Lord. She has a message for me as well: learn to receive your love, and find a way to love you back.

Alma holds out the prayer shawl to Teresa.

Teresa touches it, weeps.

As soft as I remember.

39

Sounds of a very loving guitar.

Lights slowly fade to black.

In the darkness, a haunting guitar.

Light finds Alma, composing a letter.

ALMA:

Dearest Eli, is it possible? It has been thirteen years since I first wrote to you? I have been very careful to burn your letters. You wonder how I have been able to hold our ancestor's teaching in my mind? I do not leave it to my mind. I dance Kabbalah in my body.

She illustrates with elegant movements.

Music of a soft guitar accompanies.

In dance I celebrate what you taught me: we humans co-create the divine, with our every thought, word, deed.

As she moves fluidly.

I tell the story of the sefirot: ten eternal expressions of value and being, each, hanging like a ripe fruit on the Tree of Life. But of course the tree is upside-down, for such is the life of a Jew!

Her hands reach upward.

The roots reach up, to *Ein Sof,* the "endless" . . . Are you there, Mama and Papa, in the great Nothing?

Changing rhythm, moving her feet.

My toes are the branches in this upside-down world, my feet wet with the soil of the tenth sefirah: Shekhinah, bride of God, standing at the gate, the shining light of self-knowledge, for without seeing ourselves, we can never know the other.

The dance moves to the core of her body.

Each sefirah is a world: "Wisdom"—

She dances it.

"Intelligence"—

She dances it.

"Will"—

It is seen in dance.

"Mastery"—

She dances it.

"Magnificence." All opposites must join to create divine Providence.

The dance in the core of her body becomes one of uncertainty, turmoil

I do not understand, Eli. If there is a divine plan for us, what is the way out of our suffering?

The dance builds in its expression of conflict, agony.

I am tormented by my vision of Shekhinah, torn asunder between Power, and Love. I feel Her in my own body, longing to mend, but the mending does not come.

She slows in the dance, gradually releasing her anger.

Music fades.

Sometimes, late at night, when all the world is asleep, I lie awake, longing for a love greater that my love for the Mother of Jesus; greater than my love for you, Eli, greater than anything I have ever known.

Lights fade.

Music in the darkness, a guitar of discord.

Light finds Teresa and Alma on the mule cart.

CRACK! of the whip.

TERESA:

Faster, Pablo. We are late.

ALMA:

The people of this village are so impatient?

TERESA:

The magistrate is also their bishop. He calls our Reform, "the gypsy curse."

ALMA:

The road narrows. Pablo, slow down!

TERESA:

You cannot give him orders.

ALMA:

We charge forward into the dark!

TERESA:

There is no darkness when we have our Lord. Pray with me. Saint Joseph will lead us.

ALMA:

We need a map, a fleet of torches, tell Pablo to slow down.

Teresa ignores her, makes the sign of the cross, closes her eyes.

TERESA:

> Dearest Saint Joseph, show us the way this dark night. We have no star of David. We must depend on your light.

> *(to Alma)*

> Pray, sister!

ALMA:
(exasperated)

> Saint Joseph, help us.

TERESA:

> There is no heart in your words.

ALMA:

> What, I must lift the end of each word like a nightingale? "Saint Joseph, help us."

TERESA:

> I smell a hypocrite.

ALMA:

> I pray for *you*. I do everything for *you*. It is never good enough.

TERESA:
(gasps; hearing something)

> . . . What is this? "Stop or you die!"

ALMA:

> I heard it too.

TERESA:

Pablo, stop!

Teresa and Alma respond to the "stop" of the cart.

They get out, and peer down over the lip of the stage.

A chasm. One more rotation, we would have plunged to our death.

ALMA:

(calling into the darkness)

Thank you, kind señor, you saved our lives!

TERESA:

What señor?

ALMA:

A shepherd, perhaps. I cannot see. I heard only his voice.

TERESA:

It is not *that* dark. I see no mortal.

(closing her eyes)

Thank you, Saint Joseph.

ALMA:

It was a man. Pablo heard him too.

TERESA:

Disparate! Nonsense. You are a woman of small mind, lashed to a common earth.

ALMA:

And you? Mother Teresa of Cruelty that you show to me alone.

TERESA:

Pablo, back us out of here, before sister Alma and I toss one another over the edge.

Lights shift from night to day. Alma and Teresa move the chairs of the wagon aside.

Music: triumphant.

> *Teresa walks forward, facing the audience, waving, greeting the people of the town. Alma is beside her, yet quite distant.*

TERESA:

We are honored, good people!

ALMA:

(aside, to Teresa)

No doubt they heard "Saint Joseph" saved us from the abyss.

TERESA:

(aside, to Alma)

Every miracle has its practical uses. The founding of this convent should go quite smoothly.

ALMA:

This will not appease your enemies in the church.

TERESA:

The people are God's true church.

ALMA:

Silencio! The Pope, it is said, has an elephant's ears.

Teresa is silent, seeing the wisdom in Alma's words.

Lights fade.

Music, a melancholy guitar.

Lights find Alma, alone, reading a letter she has plucked from the rope.

Teresa enters. Alma presses the letter against her breast.

TERESA:

> You are yet angry with me, that I stoop to the level of a politician?

ALMA:

> No, I am awash with quite different emotions.

TERESA:

> Have I not given you a wellspring of a mother's love? And, yes, a measure of torment into the mix, like any mother. I marvel I have loved you enough to be cruel to you by spells, forgetting, at such times, that you hold a dagger over my heart.

ALMA:

> It is a power I never wanted.

TERESA:

> I find that hard to believe. Others can boast of meekness, but you, Alma de Leon, are quite interested in power. I admire that.

ALMA:

> It does not matter now. There is nothing I can do to you the church has not already done.

Alma hands the letter to Teresa.

TERESA:
(reading)

"Teresa of Jesus, you are henceforth ordered to cease the establishment of any new Discalced Orders. All Discalced sons and daughters are declared rebellious and disobedient, most prominently you yourself. . ."

Stunned, she drops the letter.

What else?

ALMA:

Can you bear it?

TERESA:

If I can withstand the fires of the devil, I can stand this.

ALMA:

You are branded apostate, confined in solitude to the Convent of the Incarnation.

TERESA:

Back there? Where I first fled my father's house to become a nun? I know the room. No windows. I would prefer the prison of the Inquisition. There at least I would be surrounded by like-minded souls. Those behind this, in their golden robes, hate us for our modesty, our poverty, that we garner the love, and support of the people. Where are our advocates? John of the Cross? Jerónimo Gracián? The other barefoot friars?

ALMA:

They are imprisoned as well.

(delicately)

They accuse you of sexual relations with Gracián.

TERESA:

> Dear God in Heaven. We have never touched, flesh to flesh, yet I confess there is a riot of tender feelings between us. A passionate intimacy of the soul.

ALMA:

> King Philip cannot stop this?

TERESA:

> It smacks of the Vatican. Philip shivers for his immortal soul.

ALMA:

> We are all heretics now.

TERESA:

> You must return to Saint Joseph's. Let your Spouse, our Lord Christ, do His will, and you will see how, before long, the sea will swallow up those who are making war upon us, and God will free His people![6]

ALMA:

(retrieving the letter from the floor)

> There is one thing more. Is your Lord with you?

TERESA:

> Always.

ALMA:

> Hold his hand, this moment.

Teresa crosses herself, closes her eyes.

> They have declared you Excommunicate.

Teresa opens her eyes, puts her hand to her breast, breathing slowly.

TERESA:

(kneeling)

Is this your will my Lord? Do I deserve to be set adrift from your holy church on the road to Hell? If so, what is my crime?

Teresa listens, gasps, opens her eyes.

ALMA:

What is it?

TERESA:

(in the rapture)

Our Lord, ascending the cross, looking down, at me, at you. He has never appeared to me like this before, but always whole, healthy.

ALMA:

You have never been crucified, before.

TERESA:

He shows me the wounds in his hands, his feet.

ALMA:

I wish I could see Him too.

TERESA:

You do not need to see our Lord like this. You have seen enough . . . He tells me to use my imprisonment wisely.

(a wry chuckle)

Of course.

ALMA:

Will I ever see you again?

Teresa holds out her hands to Alma. They clasp hands, touch their bare toes.

They stay in this way for a moment, with great feeling.

Lights fade.

Music. A churning, discordant guitar.

Lights find Teresa, alone in a chair.

She crosses the room, addressing an offstage character.

TERESA:

Sister Jailer! Forgive me. That is unkind. Sister, please, cease this endless parade of guinea fowl and sugar cakes. We Discalced eat only milk and honey. It goes better with our bare feet! Yes, go!

Teresa turns away, smiles to herself.

I am the devil's child, secretly savoring the moist luxury of fowl in my mouth, licking the sugar from my wanton lips!

Feeling the onset of rapture, she gasps, moans.

It is You, dearest Lord, as you were upon Resurrection: wounded but healed . . . I'm to pen a new book? . . . the journey of the soul to intimacy with God . . .

She gasps, experiencing a rapture of sublime perfection. She cries out at its splendor, kneeling in consummate awe.

What is this shimmering within me? . . . A most beautiful crystal globe, in the shape of a castle . . .

She rises, in awe, moving in the rapture.

The nearer I get to the center, the stronger the light . . .[7] In the innermost chamber I have no "I." No Mother Teresa of the Melon-head . . . "I" and "You" are One.

She feels something horrible encroach on the vision.

Toads! Vipers! Snakes![8]

She sees the true face of the vermin within.

I know you: envy, greed, self-loathing, gluttony, vanity.

Teresa holds off these inner demons with the chair, as she would tame a lion.

The poison in our minds must be conquered if the soul is to approach the castle.[9] And who is this conquering "I?" No Melon-head, she is my warrior, my will. The stronger she is, the closer I can come, to You, dearest Lord . . . Ah, I must write this down!

Teresa hurries to the rope, takes down quill and parchment, and kneels before the chair, using the seat as a desk.

Alma! Alma!

A moment, realizing Alma is not here.

I need her. I miss her.

Addressing the Unseen Presence within.

Dear Lord, watch out for her. Don't let her walk barefoot in the rain. She is apt to catch a chill. If she were here, she would say, "Write it down as you just spoke it, word by word."

Teresa smiles, with courage, and begins to write.

Lights fade.

Music in the darkness. A guitar of churning energy, anxiety, and change.

Lights find Alma, in an empty room.

> *She plucks a letter from the rope, reviews it.*

ALMA:

> Dearest Eli, I am in prison, at Saint Joseph's! They said, "Too many people storm our gates. Lock her up. Admit no one." What people, you ask? People of all faiths, crying to see me, protesting the censure of our Order. My beloved Mother Teresa suffers in her own prison. She cannot help me. Eli, I cannot see the sun, the stars, the moon. I fear I will go mad.
>
> *Tossing down the letter, breathing, attempting to collect herself.*
>
> What if I were Copernicus, locked away from the sun? I would spend my time enlisting my mind, so that the moment I was set free, I would gallop to the nearest telescope and prove my theories! If I were Mother of Jesus, I would spend every moment writing . . .
>
> *To the heavens.*
>
> Are you there, Shekhinah?

Silence, to herself.

> What way for *me*, in this darkness?
>
> *Her body begins to move, quite slowly at first, then, with increasing energy, awareness, and anger, Alma dances her despair.*

Music joins her.

She dances with increasing abandon, the movements unique, alive.

At the end of the dance, lights fade.

Lights find Teresa, rolling up a letter she has plucked off the rope.

She calls off stage.

TERESA:
Sister Jailer—Pardon me, "Sister," dispatch this letter to Alma de Leon at Saint Joseph's. I want her to personally deliver it to King Philip . . . What? She is locked up in solitude as well? For what offense? . . . Basta!

Aside.

My poor Alma. The people love her, the most unpardonable sin.

Back to the offstage sister.

Then, Sister, *you* must take my letter to the King. Stand tall, woman. You cannot slouch at court! You will not be branded a heretic for delivering a message! . . . Hum, good point. Well, you must do it anyway! I make the case that Philip stands before God, not the Pope! Philip must decree that we, the *barefoot*, have our own Dominion in this churchly firmament of dust and power-lust. Go!

Teresa feels the Unseen Presence within.

My Lord, what is your will? . . . ah, yes, the book . . . You will dictate a metaphor of the soul's incubation, on its road to intimacy with You? . . . "When the warm weather comes, and the mulberry trees begin to show leaf, the silkworm feed on the mulberry leaves until they are full grown. Then, with their own tiny mouths, they start spinning silk, making them very tight little cocoons, in which they bury themselves. Then, finally, the worm, which was large and ugly, comes right out of the cocoon a beautiful white butterfly."[10]

Aside.

How I wish I could share this one with you, Alma.

Addressing the Heavens.

Dearest Alma de Leon, find your might. Do not let them conquer you.

Lights fade.

Music: a whisper of hope.

Light finds Alma, asleep on the floor of her empty prison room. She stirs, as if dreaming. Her eyes open, adjusting to the light. They open wider. She takes in breath, sitting up, looking at the empty place beside her on the floor, touches it.

ALMA:

Eli. You are not here . . . A dream. You and I were running out of a burning building. Your friend, his wife, with their baby strapped to her breast, followed us. We ran through the streets, buildings crumbling all around us, yet we were not crushed. We held onto each other . . . Then, you were here, lying beside me,

54

our bodies, one. I could feel your breath against my cheek.

Alma feels a depth of emotion, a new awareness coming to her. She rises, with increasing strength, and purpose.

Alma places her hand upon her breast, addressing an inner reality.

Shekhinah, are you the author of this dream?— Whomever you are, wherever you are, I thank you.

Music, energy, transcendence.

Alma ceremoniously takes off her veil, and leaves it coiled on the floor. She shakes her head, hair flying loose, as she creates a new dance, of freedom, joy, flight.

Lights fade.

In the darkness, the magnificence of Cathedral Bells.

Lights up on Teresa, walking downstage, her walk betraying signs of her age.

She addresses the audience, as the people of Avila, waving with great joy.

TERESA:
Open wide your windows, good people of Avila! Open your doors! God Save the King! God Save the King!

The bells chime.

Alma enters, without her veil, wearing new shoes, her prayer shawl wrapped around her. She watches Teresa, moved by the sight of her beloved Mother waving to the crowd.

Alma tosses a white flower. It lands at Teresa's feet.

Teresa sees Alma, as if in a trance. The chimes cease.

An angel tosses me white butterflies!

ALMA:

Last time I noticed. Mother, I am still alive.

TERESA:

Alma!

They seize hands.

ALMA:

They let me out. I was already free. No chains can bind the enlightened soul. You wrote that.

TERESA:

Did I? I think you dreamed it.

ALMA:

They say you are not well.

TERESA:

Should I be, at my age?

(fetching the white flower at her feet)

This did not come from a cocoon.

ALMA:
(smiling)

Almond blossoms. They litter the streets. A measure of your triumph.

TERESA:

It was our King. However did he conquer his fear of the Pope?

ALMA:

Your letters.

TERESA:

No, no he found this courage in his own self. What were your words, Alma, dearest? "Mend" and "Fight." This one precious day, our lady God, Shekhinah, is *whole*. The branches of power and loving compassion that ripped her apart are brought together, in our victory.

(smells the flower)

Magnificent . . .

(in a bustle of energy)

We have much to do! Send for Pablo! We travel tomorrow to Caravaca, Palencia—

ALMA:

Your health—

TERESA:

What of it? To die on the road would be a wonderful thing, out, among the people, the stars, the hot wind blistering our cheeks! Ah, and my new book. *The Interior Castle.* You must let me know if I have described—however imperfectly—the soul's journey to Spiritual Marriage with God.

ALMA:

I am sure it has great merit.

TERESA:

(calming, studying her closely)

> Where is your veil?

ALMA:

> I cast it off.

TERESA:

> You are wearing shoes.

ALMA:

> A gift, from the people of San Roche. Oh, Mother, when I walked out of that prison at Saint Joseph's—I stepped into a world I had never seen before. Splinters of light blinked at me from every branch of the limberbush, from every crimson blossom, reaching to the sky. Everywhere, the radiance of these splinters, in the whipping dust along the road, the swirl of a little girl's white dress. Beyond beauty.

TERESA:

> The divine light, in all things.

ALMA:

> The people ran to me, shouted for joy, gave me persimmons! I began to dance! They cheered and threw pennies. "Take these shoes!" cried an old woman, "You will need them as a dancer."

TERESA:

> You are leaving us.

ALMA:

> I want to stay with you. I want to go to my Eli.

TERESA:

> All the way to Jerusalem?

Alma nods in the affirmative.

You are not afraid?

ALMA:

I am terrified! The Turks are banishing the Jews from Jerusalem. My people are suffering. What am I to do?

TERESA:

My poor Alma. On which path lives your soul?

ALMA:

You would ask me that! How can I leave a person who wants only what is true for me?

Teresa waits. Alma faces her.

I cannot stay here cocooned in your love. I must take my place, with my own people. And, I will ask Eli to marry me.

TERESA:

A wedding! I wish I could be there.

Alma takes Teresa's hand, and walks with her.

ALMA:

After we are wed beneath a canopy of stars, we will walk out into the meadow, to welcome the return of the exiled Shekhinah, the bride of God. A place will be set for her at the wedding feast. On this night, the human and the divine become one.

Teresa reaches for Alma and embraces her.

Alma melts into her arms.

TERESA:

My daughter, my soul.

ALMA:

(with the greatest joy, the greatest loss)

My Mother—

TERESA:

(gently pulling her away)

Go, dearest. Go.

Alma hurries from the room.

Teresa looks around, quite lost. She cradles the white flower in her palm, lifts it toward the sun.

Fly, my white butterfly, fly!

Music of love and eternity.

Lights fade to black.

NOTES

1. "An angel, in bodily form . . . leaves me completely afire with a great love for God." Teresa of Avila, *The Life of Teresa of Jesus*. (New York: Image books Doubleday) 1991

2. "The devil here on my left . . . as if in despair." Avila, *The Life*.

3. "The Godhead is like a very clear diamond . . . depths of our souls." Avila, *The Life*.

4. "as many as she had hairs on her head." From Juan Bautista Rubeo, Carmelite General, 1567. Quoted in Shirley du Boulay's *Teresa of Avila An Extraordinary Life* (New York: Bluebridge) 2004.

5. "I will not have it said . . . I want you to be strong men!" Teresa of Avila. Boulay's *Teresa of Avila*.

6. "Before long the sea will rise . . . free his people." Teresa of Avila. Boulay's *Teresa of Avila*.

7. "A most beautiful crystal globe . . . stronger the light." Teresa of Avila, *The Interior Castle* (New York: Image books Doubleday) 1989.

8. "Toads, vipers, snakes" Avila, *The Interior Castle*.

9. "The poison in the mind . . . approach the castle." Avila, *The Interior Castle*.

10. "When the warm weather comes . . . white butterfly." Avila, *The Interior Castle*.

BIOGRAPHICAL AND IMAGINAL
ORIGINS OF THE PLAY

On the Doorstep of the Castle combines a dramatization of the very real historical figure, Teresa of Avila, with a fictional character, Alma de Leon. The idea for this dramatic convention came when I was researching Teresa's life and works. I saw her as the "rock star" of the Medial Woman, someone who mediates for others between heaven and earth. I wanted to place her in a story with a woman who embodied the Amazon.

I made several attempts, placing Teresa in an imagined realm in the Collective Unconscious with real historical Amazon figures. It was a miserable failure. The characters were hollow, stilted. I woke one morning and realized I was trying to be Samuel Beckett, author of *Waiting for Godot*. How very silly of me. But the writing process is always a teacher. With respect to Beckett's genius, I realized that because of who I am, I needed to place my characters in a real world context, with real struggles and challenges.

I was aware of the twentieth century Jewish philosopher, Edith Stein, who chanced to read Teresa's autobiography and realized it was what she had been searching for all her life. She converted to the Carmelite order, yet could not curb her criticism of the Pope, who turned the other way while the Jews were being led to the death camps from Italy. Her public denunciation eventually resulted in the Gestapo escorting Edith and her sister, Rosa, to Auschwitz, where they were exterminated in 1942.

I was so moved by this story I began to imagine a young Jewish woman, living in 16th century Spain, who, like Edith Stein, was searching for something to feed the longing of her soul.

"What if Teresa and Edith met?" I thought, with a sense of great excitement. I did not transpose Edith directly to the 16th century, but began to research the story of the Jews at that time. The character of Alma, Spanish for soul, emerged in vivid dreams and images from the dusty plains of central Spain.

I tossed out my preconceptions and ideas about the story, and just let the characters guide me. Alma had Edith's courage, but was not a philosopher. She was a woman of the senses, the earth, the arts. I allowed the action of the play to follow Alma's desires, as I also followed the real life events in the history of Teresa of Jesus.

Many of the raptures come from Teresa's own writing: the angel piecing her heart, the devil snarling in her ear, the vision of the crystal globe in the shape of the castle, and the metaphor of the white butterfly. In history, she was indeed ordered to take to the road and establish as many Discalced convents as "there are hairs on your head." She was imprisoned by the church when her Discalced convents threatened the established order, excommunicated, and accused of sexual relations with the Discalced monk, Jerónimo Gracián. She denied any carnal association, but the two had such a passionate friendship, after her death, Gracián cut her left ring finger from her body and wore it around his neck for the rest of his life.

These wonderful details are told brilliantly in Shirley du Boulay's biography, *Teresa of Avila: An Extraordinary Life.* In the play, many details were adapted to fit the needs of the dramatic form. In history, Teresa wrote her books on a draughty window sill. We transposed this to a chair. Teresa's beloved copy of Osuna's *Third Spiritual Alphabet* was indeed impounded by the Inquisition, and the nuns in Saint Joseph's spent their evenings singing and dancing, with Teresa composing many of the songs.

I imagined Alma as a descendent of Moses de Leon, the historical Jewish scholar who wrote *The Zohar*, the book of the Kabbalah. Of course Alma would be descended from this man, since a large part of her spiritual journey is to learn the tradition of Kabbalah, and how it applies to her path of individuation. Alma's experience of the execution of her grandfather, the expulsion of her beloved cousin Eli, her own forced conversion to Catholicism, are fictional representations of very real events. Beginning in 1492, Spanish monarchs Ferdinand and Isabella, expelled most of the Jews from Spain. The Inquisition finished the job by executing the most "rebellious," and forcing the rest to convert. Many scholarly works chronicle this story, including *A History of the Jews* by Abraham Leon Sachar, and *Jerusalem* and *A History of God* by Karen Armstrong.

Another surprise came to me as I allowed the characters to write the play: both are Amazons, both are Medial Women, both are entirely human, filled with fear, dread, shame, passion, doubt, a longing to belong, and to connect with a world larger than themselves. I developed an even greater respect for Toni Wolff's essay, *Structural Forms of the Feminine Psyche*. Her four archetypal feminine energies: Mother, Hetaira, Amazon, and Medial Woman flow through all of us, including men who are aware of these aspects of their inner anima. These energies are not mythological goddesses on a cloud. They live and breathe through our flawed, yearning humanity.

The title of the play is *On the Doorstep of the Castle*, because in my experience, this is where we find ourselves, again and again. We may enter the innermost castle, lose our inflated ego, and join with the Higher Self, but, sooner or later, a new life event, or arriving at a new developmental stage, brings us back to the doorstep. There, by fighting away Teresa's "toads, vipers, snakes," we find our courage, our will, our tireless Amazon of the soul, and She makes us whole, again and again.

It Was Meant to Be
By Lindsey Rosen

Bashert.

Yiddish for: "It was meant to be."

Fourteen years ago this fall, I sat next to my grandmother's Hospice bed to say goodbye. It was Yom Kippur, The Day of Atonement, the Holiest of Holy Days for Jews. The day when it is written in The Book of Life, who shall live, who shall die. The day we recognize it is out of our hands. Some things are already written. Some things were meant to be.

Like me, my grandmother was a twin. Like me, she was small in stature and kinetically robust; a dancer, yogini, writer; a woman who enjoyed feeding the birds, and believed one's window should always have a view .

On that day it had been written. Grandma was leaving us. She had slipped into a coma, her voice already gone.

I spoke to her.

When it was time, my sister and aunt also gathered around my grandmother.

It was the women in the family who had come to watch over grandma's death.

We didn't consciously know this was the role of women in Judaism—to tend to, care for, and prepare the dying for their transition. This was not a Jewish family.

Only I was Jewish. I had converted earlier that spring, dipping my body into a fresh water lake *mikvah* near my grandparents' Northern Michigan cottage while I recited the blessings that reconnected my Soul to its ancestral home. None of my biological relatives were Jewish, yet my spiritual compass continually pointed me in that direction.

On that day at my grandmother's bed we told stories about her, we women. My aunt had brought old newspaper clippings with photos of grandma and her twin sister in dance performances at the Pabst Theatre in Milwaukee, Wisconsin. My grandmother loved to tell stories about her childhood on the stage: the elaborate costumes, the colorful characters, the gold gilded ceiling and red velvet seats. The dancing, performing twin girls were adored by their stepfather, Albert, an actor, director and manager of the Pabst Theatre. I had heard these stories many times, always told with a deep love and wistful yearning for the past life, the only father they knew, who died too early.

What I hadn't heard before, or didn't remember hearing, was that Albert was Jewish.

Like me, the most important man in my grandmother's life was a Jew.

Albert's troupe was a Yiddish Theatre troupe, at a time when Milwaukee's German community was highly segregated between Jews and non-Jews. He had fallen in love with and married my great grandmother, adopted her 3 children as his own, and used theater as his voice to bridge that divide in the community. Albert's early death, the heightened tensions of WWII, and my great grandmother's grief separated my grandmother from that world.

My aunt told us that grandma had been dreaming about that time in her life, before the coma. She was troubled that her mother hadn't done enough to help Jewish troupe members get their families out of Nazi Germany during the war. It was haunting her as she prepared to leave this world.

Perhaps I am bridging some divide in the family collective.

I shared with my aunt that I had recently converted and hadn't known that Albert was Jewish. She told me she had something for me, something grandma had given her, something my great grandmother had given grandma, something Albert had given my great grandmother.

It was a gold Star of David necklace, with tiny rubies and a pearl in the center, my birthstone. On the backside is great grandmother's name: Alma.

Alma means soul.

This year, I make my acting debut in Elizabeth Clark-Stern's new play *On the Doorstep of the Castle*. Though I have performed many times on stage, I have been a dancer, finding my voice through my body's movement, as my grandmother did. Now I will claim a spoken voice. My own voice and that of my character's: a 16th Century young Jewish woman, ripped apart from her family during the Inquisition, forced to convert to Catholicism, searching for her spiritual home, and a way to integrate all that has come before her and all that will ever be. A woman who is attempting to bridge divides—between her past and her future, her biological family and her spiritual family, the spiritual masculine and the feminine.

I too am bridging divides.

And so it was written in The Book of Life. I am to find my voice on the stage. I am to play this character who embodies traces of my own soul searching.

My character's name? Alma.

Bashert.

It was meant to be.

To order Fisher King titles call
toll free within Canada and the U.S.
1-800-228-9316
International calls
+1-831-238-7799

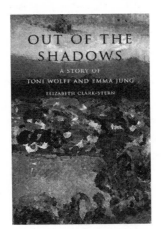

Out of the Shadows
A Story of Toni Wolff and Emma Jung
by Elizabeth Clark-Stern
ISBN 978-1926975009

The year is 1910. Sigmund Freud and his heir-apparent, Carl Jung, are changing the way we think about human nature and the mind. Twenty-two year old Toni Wolff enters the heart of this world as Jung's patient. His wife, Emma Jung, is twenty-six, a mother of four, aspiring to help her husband create the new science of psychology. Toni Wolff's fiercely curious mind, and her devotion to Jung, threaten this aspiration. Despite their passionate rivalry for Jung's mind and heart, the two women often find themselves allied. Born of aristocratic Swiss families, they are denied a university education, and long to establish themselves as analysts in their own right. Passionate and self-educated, they hunger for another intellectual woman with whom to explore the complexities of the soul, the role of women in society, and the archetypal feminine in the affairs of nations.

Their relationship spans 40 years, from pre-World War I to the dawn of the Atomic Age. Their story follows the development of the field of psychology, and the moral and professional choices of some of its major players. Ultimately, Toni and Emma discover that their individual development is informed by both their antagonism, and their common ground. They struggle to know the essence of the enemy, the other, and to claim the power and depth of their own nature.

il piccolo editions is an imprint of Fisher King Press.
Learn more about many other worthy publications at:
www.fisherkingpress.com